Helping with LIFE TRANSITIONS

Engaging YOUNG ADULTS with DISABILITIES into the LIFE OF YOUR CHURCH

Mike Dobes

THE IRRESISTIBLE CHURCH SERIES

Joni and Friends

Helping with Life Transitions
Print: ISBN 978-1-946237-23-1
Kindle: ISBN 978-1-946237-24-8
EPUB: ISBN 978-1-946237-25-5

Author: Mike Dobes
Contributing Author: Ryan Wolfe
Collaborators: Rick McLean, Jeff McNair
Contributing Editor: Ali Howard
Editor-in-Chief: Eric Jones

Printed in the United States of America

Produced by The Denzel Agency (www.denzel.org)
Cover and Interior Design: Rob Williams

For information, rights and permissions, or to order additional print copies of this and other resources, contact the publisher:

Joni and Friends International Disability Center
P.O. Box 3333, Agoura Hills, California 91376-3333
Email: churchrelations@joniandfriends.org
Phone: 818-707-5664

Kindle version available at www.irresistiblechurch.org

CONTENTS

Introduction

Mike Dobes, co-author of this book, clearly remembers the day that his daughter was born. All the moments leading up to her birth, and her actual birth, are firmly etched in his memory—even down to the detail that she was born in the same hospital where his father was born. Talk about a cool legacy story! The busyness of the nurses and the doctor, the expert coaching that he received, and their family waiting eagerly outside the room, all culminated with a final moment. His daughter was born! Mike was able to cut her umbilical cord, wrap her in a blanket, and hold her briefly before she was whisked away by the medical staff to check her basic stats and vitals. The days and months that followed were spent feeding her, changing her diapers, bathing her, and lots of family naps. A truly life-transforming event!

Now, fifteen years later, the way that he continues to care for and look out for her has changed drastically. She is now seeking her identity in Christ, learning how to stand against the crowd, and trying to decide what she wants to be when she enters adulthood. Mike now acts more as a listener and counselor than as a director. His heart for her, his prayers over her, and his desire to see her succeed have only increased since she was born. But how he expresses these things must constantly change to meet her age-appropriate needs. Adjusting parenting strategy and style is necessary as time passes—a reality that every parent faces, regardless of the culture you live in or the ability level of your children.

Unfortunately, many churches approach disability ministry as if it is something that is frozen in time. Whether it is intentional or not, most churches make their children's ministry responsible for any efforts related to disability ministry. Perhaps it is easier for volunteers and leaders to envision themselves serving cute babies and young children with Down syndrome rather than adults with cognitive delays. Perhaps churches are tight on resources, and staff members have a very small margin for any additional programs. Both authors of this book spent many years as youth pastors, so they understand the mindset that if you serve children well, their parents and extended family will often participate in the life of the church. Regardless of the reason, the difficult reality is that disability ministry programming doesn't often exist outside of a children's ministry buddy program, leaving many of our young adult or adult friends affected by disability without a place to belong in the local church.

Children affected by disability don't stay children forever. And in the same way that parents must adjust their parenting strategies, so too our churches must adapt ministry strategies to appropriate age levels and expectations in order to serve people affected by disability well. We hope that this book will encourage more people to engage in ministry with youth or adults affected by disability. It is our desire to see churches become irresistible—places of authentic community that compel people of all ages affected by disability to fully belong.

Considering Ministry Logistics

Transitions

During our many years on full-time church staff, we were both privileged to serve a variety of age groups. Ryan is quick to say that in his many areas of responsibility, transitions were always a key component. Whether it was preparing upper-elementary kids for the different culture that youth ministry would present, or reassuring nervous parents that high school youth group was a healthy and godly place, transitions were critical. If transitions were not handled well, people could get hurt, families would become offended, and, depending upon the severity, church attendance might drop. Transitions in any environment—ministry, jobs, or personal—do not happen well without intentionality.

Transitions are difficult for most people, but this is especially true for our friends with disabilities. As you work to transition your friends from the children's ministry to the youth ministry or from the youth ministry to the adult ministry, you will inevitably experience challenges. Trusted routines developed over the years can be difficult for anyone to change. Most children's ministries evolve into youth ministries that are filled with high-energy games, loud worship, and other factors that could cause stimulus overload. Youth ministry typically evolves into adult ministry where the Bible study is deeper and the focus shifts from short, entertaining lessons to more involved discussions.

As you consider all the moving parts of ministry dynamics, family dynamics, and the effects of disability, please never lose sight of why you do what you do. Ministry is all about people! It is about relationships and providing environments and conversations that bring people into an awareness of and dependence upon Christ. It is important to take time to listen to parents or caregivers and hear their concerns and fears. Listen to your friends affected by disability and discover what is most meaningful to them in ministry. Listen to ministry leaders, Sunday school teachers, youth group volunteers, and adult ministry advocates to learn their wisdom, hesitations, and dreams.

As you approach transitions you will need to be creative and unafraid to try new things. One of your greatest resources will be information. As you begin to prepare for any transition with your friends, seek out as much information as you can find. If your friend is of school age, consider asking to see his or her current Individualized Education Plan (IEP). An IEP is a tailored, strategic plan to help your friend succeed at school. You may be thinking to yourself, *This isn't school. Why would I need that?* Professionally trained educators work hard daily with the same friend you see only once a week. Over the course of years, they have developed a plan that helps your friend be successful. Reviewing this IEP can give you great insight and understanding into what makes your friend most comfortable and what will draw the best response from him or her. To gain access to this document, you will need to respectfully ask permission from your friend's parents or caregivers. If they are willing to give you access to it, it may give you information that will help make transitions smoother because you can bring more consistency between your friend's school, home, and ministry experiences.

If your friend is past the age of school and does not have specialized educators and therapists creating an IEP for them, they will likely still have parents or caregivers who can offer a wealth of information.

In several of the Irresistible Church books, we mention having parents and caregivers complete an information sheet📚 when their loved one begins attending your ministry. As you approach a transition, you can consult this sheet, and you can also reconnect with that parent or caregiver to talk through the transition. Perhaps they can help prepare your friend at home while you work with your friend at church.

Consistency is king. What if you could provide the same expectations and support on Sunday that your friend gets Monday through Friday? When everyone works together, good things happen. Please don't ever be afraid to ask for help.

Making the decision on *when* your friend should transition is a difficult question to consider. While some people feel the need to consider what they perceive to be the mental age of an individual for teaching purposes, you should never allow this to be your criteria on ministry placement for your friends. For example, if you have a friend who is 18 years old, he has lived 18 years of life. That life experience should be respected. You should consider his emotional,

📚 This symbol indicates that there are supplemental resources that correspond with this topic at http://irresistiblechurch.org/library/

physical, and spiritual maturity as well. Emotionally, he enjoys hanging out with people his own age and seems to become more agitated when interacting with young children. He is physically strong and could accidentally cause harm to a child much smaller than himself. Spiritually, he loves the Lord. And while it takes intentional teaching for him to understand a lesson, he has a hunger to learn more. By considering his *whole* person, it might become clear that the youth ministry is actually the best fit for him at this time.

Another critical component of transitions is communication between leaders. It does not matter if you have a small team of volunteers or a large team of paid staff, without intentionality in this area, transitions are at a much higher risk of failure. We hope that someday, individuals with disabilities will be naturally integrated throughout all activities of the church, requiring less intentional efforts. But for now, we need to plan for the integration of youth and adults. A good place to start could be developing a position statement about how the leaders of your church see adults affected by disability integrating into church life—even a simple statement that could be reiterated in a variety of places, such as, "We believe all members of the body of Christ belong together.

Specifically, we endeavor to integrate persons with disabilities in all aspects of church life. Let's seek to love our neighbors in this way as a witness to ourselves and the community." A statement like this coming from church leadership could do a great deal to encourage integration in the congregation. It is one thing for such a statement to come from those leading a disability ministry, but it is quite another for it to come from those not directly involved. This type of leadership can change the social environment of the church and help create a more inclusive environment.

When an individual affected by disability makes a transition at school, teachers and therapists meet several times to transfer knowledge and get to know the student. Why should church be any different? As your friends transition from the children's ministry to the youth ministry or from the youth ministry to the adult ministry, we encourage you to take the time to bridge the gap. Have a meeting, or several! You might consider inviting the parents or caregivers of your friend as well as any key leaders of each ministry to attend the meeting. Making this effort will only help to set your friend up for a better chance at having a successful transition.

Successful transitions and belonging go beyond the preparation that is done by leadership, families, volunteers, and your friends affected by disability. It also includes other individuals at your church who are not affected by disability. Doing disability awareness and etiquette training is a great idea that will help make the entire ministry and church feel like a welcoming environment. You can also engage typical peers in your ministry to serve your friends by being a buddy.

It cannot be overstated that one of the most critical components of successful transitions is creating a positive change in the social environment. As an Irresistible Church, our goal is to teach the local body of Christ to see people with disabilities as people first. We want our friends to be seen as regular church members because that is what they are! They should have access to everything that other members have access to. They should have access to regular Bible studies, social events, and the supports that many people need throughout their lives. We are endeavoring to create cultural change within the church through the way people are perceived and included. This cultural, congregational change will lead to better transitions for those with disabilities as they enter adulthood as their needs are understood as typical and common rather than "special." To be thought of as special is not always good. Most people would prefer to be thought of as just like everyone else rather than as different, other, or special.

Environment

Analyzing your ministry environment will not only aid with transitions, but it can also help your friends become more involved on a weekly basis. Each ministry geared toward a specific age range will make a concerted effort to look, feel, and sound different. The children's program will probably be structured, colorful, and secure. A youth ministry might be more free-flowing, darker, and louder. An adult ministry is brighter, quieter, and offers the most independence.

The free-flowing, loud environment of youth ministry can be hard for some teens affected by disability to integrate into. Individuals affected by disability often have an extreme response to sensory stimuli in their environment. Each individual will respond to the environment in a unique way. Flashing lights and loud music during worship may cause one teen to have a seizure or go running out the door while others may love and thrive in this environment. They may even come to crave the loud beat of the music pulsing in their ears and the physical sensation of jumping to the music. One friend in an adult ministry might love sitting at a table talking about the Bible and how it applies to their life, while others may need more of a kinetic activity to keep their attention engaged.

Because the response of each person can be vastly different, it can be difficult if not impossible to create the "perfect" ministry environment. We would suggest that the answer instead is to equip everyone with the tools necessary for success. Gaining a thorough knowledge of your friends and what makes them thrive is a great place to begin. If any of your friends are struggling with challenging behavior, we encourage you to download the Irresistible Church book *Responding with Compassion.*

Another aspect to consider regarding your ministry environment is location. You've probably heard the phrase "location, location, location!" when it comes to the value of real estate. This maxim can also be true when it comes to your maturing friends and their ability to find belonging in the church. Specifically, this relates to time and place. Our friends should be in the places where others in the congregation frequent, at the same times that the others are there. This kind of integration might seem obvious, but unfortunately it isn't always so.

If at all possible, your ministry should not be in a place of seclusion. Tucked away in the back corner of the church building, your ministry and thereby your friends will often be overlooked. Because our goal is for all our friends to find a place of belonging in the body of Christ, we should position our ministries accordingly. If you choose to have a class for youth or adults affected by disability, we suggest that it is visible and easily accessed. This will communicate value to your friends, grow awareness, and foster a sense of belonging.

If your friends enjoy attending the main worship service, they should not be ushered into a specific section of the worship center or sanctuary. We don't ask people of the same hair color or age range to sit together, and in the same way your friends ought to be free to sit where they feel most comfortable. Because this may mean that your pastor or other church members will need an extra measure of patience and grace, we suggest holding a church-wide disability awareness training. As you think about the training, it can be helpful to ask yourself, "How can we make it easier for people to do the right thing?"

Jeff McNair and Bryan McKinney wrote an insightful article called "Social Ramps."[1] In it they talk about how to facilitate social change within a church. Using the example of a person with autism attending, it might begin with preparing the congregation. The pastor could say, "I want you to know that we are going to begin seeing more people with various disabilities attending our worship service—in particular, some persons with autism. We are so happy they are coming and look forward to the ways in which they will bless us with their participation." The pastor can then say at the same or a later date, "Let me tell you about the experience of persons with autism and their families. Do you know that they often experience significant social isolation? Individuals with autism have that experience; however, family members may as well. Families may also choose to separate themselves because they don't want to be a burden to others or may want to avoid the feeling of rejection they've experienced, and that breaks my heart. We want to come alongside those individuals and their families to love and support them. But please understand that this will cause us to make some changes in our church."

In saying these things, the pastor has helped prepare and educate the congregation. At this point, when individuals with autism and their families attend the church, people in the congregation are actually anticipating them! Perhaps people will go out of their way to interact with them as they have been prepared. According to McNair and McKinney, a final aspect of social ramps is coaching people in their interactions. Leaders of the church can help the congregation by reinforcing their efforts and the good things they are doing while also providing kind guidance when necessary. Doing this type of intentional preparation will help your goal of full inclusion be more successful. We suggest being proactive with these conversations and trainings—you don't want to wait until it becomes a perceived problem.

Style

One of the questions that ministry leaders often wrestle with is "Should we do a full-inclusion program with buddies *or* should we offer a self-contained classroom for our disability ministry?" Our suggestion is to structure your ministry with intentionality and do what is best for the families attending your church. In an ideal situation, you might be able to offer both or a hybrid program that allows your friends to enjoy fellowshipping with their peers who do not have disabilities but that also allows them a space that meets their sensory needs if they need a break from the mainstream ministry environment.

Calvary Chapel of Costa Mesa has an adult disability ministry led by Gary Lyles that provides a great example of what an adult disability ministry might look like. They meet every Sunday morning for a time of fellowship. Their service includes worship, the collection of an offering, biblical teaching, and prayer. They are also intentional to do communion once a month. They gladly welcome people of all abilities and have a wide range of ages from young adult to elderly.

For more details and training resources concerning ministry environment styles, please check out the other Irresistible Church books in this series. We recommend reading *Pathways to Belonging*, a training resource on classroom styles and setups, as well as *Call Me Friend*, a training resource for establishing a one-on-one buddy ministry at your church.

With that being said, we would like to offer one more thought for consideration. Regardless of where your friends initially feel the most comfortable, you should always be working with them toward a greater degree of inclusion. While the process is never clear and is generally messy, the goal should always be to integrate your friends in the local body of Christ in a significant way. Regardless of which style you choose to implement, remember that we are trying to create social change within the congregation so that it is a more loving and inclusive environment. We cannot emphasize enough that each of us is created with a desire to fully belong. We want to be loved, embraced, cared for, and missed when we are absent. A disability in no way removes this desire, and it is up to the church to create authentic communities where individuals can connect and truly engage in the journey of life together.

Note

1. https://www.joniandfriends.org/media/uploads/jcid/social_ramps.pdf

Assessing Your Attitude

Never Give Up

What if it just isn't working? What if a youth or adult just isn't having any success finding a place to fully belong in your church? When is it okay to give up? When is it okay to say that maybe your church just isn't the right environment for this individual? Barring an extreme situation, we would suggest that the answer is never! Never give up! Never stop trying something new.

Consider Thomas Edison. In the records of history, he is honored as an inventor with huge successes. His inventions revolutionized society and changed our world. But let's stop and take a closer look. You could also say that Thomas Edison was a colossal failure. He failed somewhere around 1,000 times before he successfully patented the incandescent light bulb. When asked about his numerous failures, he responded by saying something like, "I didn't fail 1,000 times. I've just found 1,000 ways that don't work!"

Sometimes disability ministry is like Thomas Edison and the light bulb—we must try another way when our previous ideas didn't work. Allow us to share an example of how this played out for one young lady with disabilities struggling to find belonging at her church.

This young woman, we'll call her Kinzie, desperately wanted to connect with her peers but struggled to do so in a meaningful way. She observed all the other teens in the ministry communicating with each other by using their phones. They were texting one another and responding to each others' social media posts (yes, they were in the same room as each other–it's the way of youth these days!). She wanted so badly to be like her peers, and her inability to connect like them was causing her to exhibit challenging behaviors, resulting in frustration for her and those around her. Simply having a buddy sit beside her during worship wasn't going to fix Kinzie's situation.

You might be tempted to shake your head and say that it's ridiculous that young people can't put down their phones and communicate with others face to face. We get that. But do your best to set that temptation aside and dive into the world of this teen girl.

When the ministry leader was asked, "Does Kinzie have a phone?" she responded by saying, "She had her phone taken away because of what she was doing with it." Another road block. Don't give up. It was time to get creative! The next question we asked was, "Does the youth ministry or any of the leaders have an iPad Kinzie can use?" This time we got a positive response and thought it might be the start of a solution. We wanted to honor Kinzie's parents and their desire to revoke her phone privileges, but we wanted to facilitate her ability to connect with her peers. We suggested that with the approval of Kinzie's parents, this ministry leader should download a free texting app onto an iPad that could be monitored by leadership but used by Kinzie during youth ministry. Using this device, she could still text all her friends and other leaders in the room. While this didn't solve every component of helping this young lady find a place of belonging, it was certainly a great step in the right direction. It stopped her from giving up on church and walking away.

Another way of thinking about this is to take small steps. At Joni and Friends, we have embraced the idea of "What would be better?" We begin with a clear vision in mind and assess where we are in reference to that vision. We then ask ourselves, "What would be better?" and take that small step. For example, let's say a church with a ministry that includes adults with intellectual disabilities meets on Wednesday nights. This church then asks, "What would be better?" Well, perhaps the meeting could be changed to Sunday night so that they at least meet on the same day as the rest of the congregation. And perhaps a youth group also meets on Sunday nights, allowing for some level of integration. They have taken a small step. They then ask again, "What would be better?" Perhaps the ministry that includes adults could meet after the other activities of Sunday morning (worship, Sunday school, etc.) so that people can see each other in passing. Once this level of change and integration is well accepted, they might ask again, "What would be better?" They may choose to change the meeting time for this ministry to the same time that others meet at church on Sunday mornings. This becomes the norm for the ministry. Once again the church may ask, "What would be better?" The pastor may decide to use the social ramp idea previously described to prepare the congregation for the presence of these previously isolated folks in the regular worship service with everyone else. By taking small steps, with a vision in mind, this church has continually moved toward their desired vision.

Ministry With & By

Too often, ministry is viewed as a spectator sport or as a commodity to be consumed. But this is not how God intended it to be. Ephesians 4:12 offers a definition for what ministry is meant to do: "to equip the saints for the works of ministry, for building up the body of Christ." In this verse, Paul simply says that the purpose of ministry is to "equip the saints." There are no qualifiers on this verse and can therefore be understood to include people of all abilities. This means that all people, including those affected by disability, should be equipped to minister to others for the purpose of building one another up. We understand that this is easier said than done, so let's take a look at what this means and how it might look on a practical level.

The starting point is always presence. For those with very severe disabilities, that may be a critical aspect of their gifting. Their presence causes things to change, things to be revealed in those around them. We see this clearly illustrated in the story of the Good Samaritan (see Luke 10:25-37). The man who was beaten and left for dead did nothing as those around him passed by. According to the story, he didn't call out for help. He was simply there—isolated and dying.

Yet his mere presence revealed the character of those around him.

Similarly, Henri Nouwen, author and priest who spent many years pastoring the L'Arche Daybreak Community in Canada, spoke openly about his friendship with a young man named Adam. Adam could not speak or even move without assistance, yet Nouwen wrote of his friend that he "was no longer a stranger to me. He was becoming a friend and a trustworthy companion, explaining to me by his very presence what I should have known all along: that what I most desire in life—love, friendship, community, and a deep sense of belonging—I was finding with him" (*Adam: God's Beloved*, p. 49).

So, as a starting point, we want to ensure that people with all kinds of disabilities are physically present. Once we have surrounded ourselves with individuals who are differently abled, we can consider one of the most widely used approaches to disability ministry: doing ministry *with* our friends. This truly is a great place to start as we believe doing ministry *with* people affected by disability is a better approach than ministering *to* or *for* them.

When you minister *with* an individual affected by disability, the focus shifts from disability to ability.

Your friend is no longer identified by his or her disability or by what he or she cannot do. As you build friendships with people, you can identify what they love doing, what makes them unique, and how they can play a role in the body of Christ. Discovering, developing, and deploying gifts in your friends is a critical component of doing ministry with them. Every single one of your friends is uniquely made by God on purpose for a purpose. It is an exciting privilege to walk with our friends as we help them discover how God is calling them to serve the body.

In the same way that a young man needs his father to drive with him while learning the rules of the road, we may need to serve with our friends until they build the skills and confidence to serve independently. There is a wonderful step-by-step model to help launch your friends into ministry that goes like this:

- I do; you watch.
- We do.
- You do; I watch.
- You do.

A simple way to picture this model is through the eyes of a child. Children learn from their parents initially by simply watching. Take, for example, learning how to roller-skate. After watching her father, a young girl expresses the desire to skate. Typically, when you attend a family skate night, you will see parents slowly moving around the rink with their arms wrapped around little children struggling to maintain balance. Eventually, they begin to figure out how to skate and they need less hands-on guidance. You may even see a young child adamantly tell her parents to let her do it herself. As the lesson continues, the parents shift into watching mode, and it is not long until the child is off skating solo without the need for additional guidance. However, when she falls, there is an instant cry for assistance, and a good parent is always within range.

So, what does this look like in disability ministry? Let's examine a scenario where your friend affected by disability wants to become a greeter for the church.

As we mentioned previously, preparing and educating the congregation that there will be those with disabilities serving as greeters is a great place to begin. Some of our friends with disabilities may have appearances or social skills that are unfamiliar and daunting to some members of the congregation. By preparing the congregation, you will help ensure the success of your friends as they serve.

Once you have prepared the congregation, you can begin modeling what a greeter looks and acts like for your friend. Perhaps for several weeks, you become a greeter at the door while your friend stands nearby, observes, and is encouraged to ask questions about what he sees. You can talk about what makes sense to him, what is confusing, and what he would do differently. Next, you would serve *with* your friend as greeters for the church; perhaps you could both flank either side of the same door. This can be a great time of growth and excitement for your friend as he is taking baby steps into ministry service. As you serve together, continue engaging your friend in questions, instruction, and encouragement as needed.

After some time, you will reach a point where your friend is ready to serve on his own. As he steps into this ministry position, you can step back to observe how he is doing. You might provide small redirections, ideas, or enthusiastic encouragement, but he is now skating on his own while keeping you within arms' reach.

The final step would be completely releasing your friend to serve as an official greeter while you return to other ministry responsibilities, or even begin mentoring a new friend. As in our roller-skating example, it is wise to make yourself available in case of emergencies or simply for some well-timed encouragement and appreciation. Once this cycle is complete, you can begin the process with someone else, or perhaps even help your friend begin mentoring someone else who also wants to be a greeter.

Throughout this process you are partners in ministry together. And while your friend may need close attention and assistance along the way, you will hopefully reach a point where your friend can serve independently.

Independence is an important ideal for almost everyone. This is no different for young adults and adults affected by disability. In light of that, let's take the concept of doing ministry *with* our friends and push it a bit further. As our friends gain confidence doing ministry with us, they will hopefully transition to doing ministry on their own. This means ministry is being conducted *by* our friends with disabilities.

When ministry is done by individuals affected by disability, they have a greater sense of ownership in their service, and they become more involved in the life of the church. There are simple areas of ministry that can be done by those with intellectual or other types of disabilities. For some, greeting or collecting the offering is no big deal, no challenge. For others, serving in this way challenges their abilities and is a significant honor. One such gentleman associated with Joni and Friends can tell you exactly the number of times he was allowed to take the offering (currently it has been 17 times). For him, to be given the opportunity to serve by collecting the offering is an honor, something that he is significantly blessed to do. Asking individuals with disabilities to serve in a way that is challenging to them might actually encourage those with more ability to take on areas of service that stretch them too. Gary Lyles, from Calvary Chapel of Costa Mesa, often talks about his friends who help lead worship on Sunday mornings. A young man named Jared often plays his ukulele while Michael plays the piano. In addition to these musicians, a woman named Carol frequently leads the class in sign language to "Jesus Loves Me." By focusing on the gifts and talents of these individuals rather than on their disabilities, they are able to engage in ministry and be an encouragement to others.

To fully belong means that you are an active participant in community and that you are missed when you are unable to attend. Belonging goes beyond sharing space in a church facility—it means that significant relationships have been formed and that you have a place to share your God-given gifts.

We feel strongly that as ministry leaders it is our job to create safe environments where people can discover their gifts and be released into ministry. There are many ways within the church that ministry can be done by our friends. The following list offers a small sampling of ways that your friends could engage in ministry:

Ministry Opportunities in the Church

- Greeter
- Usher
- Communion or offering server
- Technology assistant (i.e., running PowerPoint slides, operating a camera, setting up worship-team equipment)
- Buddy for a younger friend with a disability
- Children's ministry assistant
- Cafê volunteer
- Security team assistant
- Parking lot team volunteer

- Prayer leader during adult, youth, or children's worship
- Choir member
- Sign-language leader
- Facility team member (i.e., stacking chairs, cleaning, set-up)

Something to consider with ministry opportunities is the reality that some of the roles or responsibilities might need to be adapted to allow for your friend affected by disability to serve according to her ability. This might mean that somebody without the use of her hands could greet and seat people as an usher but would need a partner to assist with handing out bulletins or giving communion. Would you be willing to allow somebody who uses a wheelchair to join the parking lot team? A friend who is non-verbal could still serve in the café as long as he feels safe to communicate in his own unique way.

Ministry opportunities must be more about relationship and serving than about accomplishment and task delegation. Emily Colson talks about her church and how they opened their doors wide to her son Max, who has autism, when he wanted to join the Grunt Crew. This crew stacks the chairs and vacuums the church sanctuary every Sunday after service so that the space is ready for youth group. Max enthusiastically began helping and was officially invited to join the team. He was not asked to change who he was but was provided a place to serve that brought incredible joy to himself, his mom, and to the entire church. In Emily's words, "God has a mission for Max at our church, backward as it may once have appeared. Max doesn't just come to church; he's part of the church." He has never sat through a service; instead he worships and dances at the back of the sanctuary until it's time to serve. "Max's joy of worship is so pure and free that it feels as though someone sprayed air freshener all around us. As Paul [the senior pastor] says, 'Church isn't over until Max dances at the back door'" (*Dancing with Max*, pp. 163-164).

Is this not how every church should be? A place where people gather, serve and exercise their gifts according to their abilities, and bring God glory in all that they do? I don't know about you, but that sounds pretty irresistible!

And while the church is a great place for gifts to be discovered and developed, people affected by disability should also be encouraged to take their ministry beyond the walls of the church. Some of the ways that we have seen ministry by young adults affected by disability in our community include but are not limited to the following:

Ministry Opportunities Outside the Church

- Leading a Bible study at a local fast-food restaurant
- Creating devotionals
- Inviting friends to church
- Volunteering in the community
- Making and sharing a meal with friends and neighbors in need
- Donating food, toys, and clothing
- Being a prayer warrior
- Using musical talents to bless others
- Offering encouragement to others
- Using artistic talents to bless others
- Coaching sports
- Collecting books for local libraries or hospitals

For youth and adults affected by disability to truly belong, they must not only discover their giftedness but also should be empowered to deploy those gifts. It is at this point that they stop being an object of ministry and instead become the minister. Ministry opportunities outside of the church are endless and should reflect the passions, skills, and hearts of the people in your church. I would encourage you to not limit opportunities based on what the church has always done before. By opening your church doors a little bit wider to new perspectives and ideas, you might be amazed by how God will use your friend affected by disability to change the trajectory of your church. This is part of Max's mission at his church, and there are people with the same mission for your church who are just waiting to be invited into authentic community.

Living Life Together

The difference between a good ministry and a great ministry isn't what happens during ministry programming. What makes a great ministry has more to do with what happens outside of programming. Or, in other words, it is all about building relationships. Do people care about having a quality program? Absolutely! But, at the end of the day, an amazing program isn't as important for most people as knowing that the leadership or members of the church care about them. People will eagerly attend a mediocre program if they know the leader is personally invested in their lives. On the other hand, an amazing program will only keep people engaged for a short time if it becomes clear that the leaders really do not care about them.

So, how can we build quality relationships with our friends and show them that we care for them? We would suggest taking time to invest in them outside your ministry and doing so on a regular basis. Why? Because that is what friends do. This might mean attending their sports games or extracurricular activities. It might mean attending your friend's birthday celebration or sharing a meal with her and her family. It could simply be enjoying coffee together at church, or buying a donut and having a conversation for 15 minutes. A weekly phone call or regular lunch date is also very much appreciated. Other ministry leaders may decide to hold a smaller mid-week Bible study with their friends in addition to Sunday morning, allowing their friends another opportunity for Christ-centered fellowship. Gary Lyles shared with us that he leads an in-home Bible study for adults with special needs. They meet at an apartment building that rents primarily to people affected by disability. Gary said that their time together is all about fellowship: "That is what we do. We share life. Not only do we share life in our daily circumstances, but we also share the life of Christ."

As you spend time with your friends, we have full confidence that while you will make an impact on their lives, you too will be profoundly encouraged and influenced by your friends.

Navigating Social Dynamics

Understanding the Family

For families affected by disability, life can often be quite difficult. Parents and caregivers spend an incredible amount of energy trying to juggle all their responsibilities while loving their family as best as they can. Many daily chores that may take a typical family a few minutes to complete can take a family affected by disability hours to accomplish. A family member with autism might find it extremely challenging to leave the comfort of their pajamas to dress, eat breakfast, and transition to the car each morning. An adult family member with limited mobility will need to be transferred, bathed, and fed before his family can leave the house. Medications need to be monitored. New therapies need to be researched and scheduled. The extracurricular activities of typical siblings need to be aligned with doctor appointments, therapy appointments, and education consultation appointments. At bedtime, many of the morning challenges are repeated. When both parents are home, they may tag-team the work, but by the end of the day there is rarely time to breathe, let alone talk. It should be no surprise that families affected by disability tend to be exhausted and often lack the energy to develop outside relationships.

Families affected by disability may also grieve the future they had once imagined. Every family experiences significant milestones over time. Parents watch their teenager transition into young adulthood as they begin college and move out of the home. Parents are proud as their adult children get new jobs, marry, and have their own children. The nest at home is now empty or at least emptier. This is the typical experience.

For families that have watched their teenagers affected by disability grow into young adults, the experience is often different. Instead of graduating at 18 years old, teens affected by disability will often stay in the high school environment for a few more years. While some will go to college, most will have different experiences. The "empty nest" is more metaphorical for families affected by disability. The comfortable nest has been, to this point, an extended school experience where they have seen their children cared for and prepared for the next chapter of life. But then it becomes time for life after school. This time of being pushed out of the nest is often full of anxiety. What comes next? Jobs? Day programs? Nothing? Families might wrestle with whether their adult children should continue living at home or move into a group home to give them more independence. By offering a place of belonging and stability, the church can play a significant role in the life of families with young adults affected by disability.

One of the greatest fears experienced by parents with children affected by disability is how their child will manage after they are gone. What happens with finances, medical concerns, jobs, and social interactions? Depending upon the severity of the disability, some of your youth and adult friends might find themselves completely dependent upon others. The church can become a wonderful place of support, encouragement, and peace for parents as they learn that their children are part of something bigger than themselves. When parents have assurance that people other than themselves care about the well-being of their children, a tremendous burden is lifted from their shoulders.

It is helpful for parents to understand that ministry done well creates a lifelong environment of friendship and support for their family member with disabilities. When people become integrated into a church, they are in a social environment that will receive them when they transition to adulthood. They are known, like anyone else, with all their strengths and quirks. We recognize that the church generally does not see itself in this way, but we are hoping and praying that we can begin to shift the vision and culture of the local church to embrace this identity. The church ought to see itself as the safety net, the link to all types of supports, the unpaid friend who can be depended upon. The local church consists of the people who visit your home, know where you work, look in your refrigerator or even your closet to ensure that you have the food and clothing you need. They will visit you in the hospital and allow you to stay at their home should you need some short-term support. Perhaps they are willing to supplement your rent and facilitate medical care when you cannot afford it. Churches must learn to see themselves in this way if we hope to create environments where people of all abilities fully belong.

Developing Authentic Community

Building relationships with your friends outside of your ministry will undoubtedly make your ministry time together richer. These efforts will also go well beyond your friends. Many individuals affected by disability have grown up their entire lives without being invited to a birthday party, asked out on a date, or invited to social functions. This is a difficult reality not only for your friend but also for their parents or caregivers. Parents experience different cycles of grief as they watch their children grow and as they watch their children's peers move into new stages of life while their own remain in a season that seems to never end. If you take the time to build relationships with youth or adults affected by disability, you will also bless their parents in uncountable ways. If you do not personally have time to invest in all the friends involved with your ministry, enlist the help of your volunteers. The effort is well worth it; the impact you can have through personal relationships is life changing.

While the topic of building authentic community is dealt with more specifically in *Doing Life Together*, we would like to briefly mention a few basic things your church can do to develop genuine fellowship. One of the most common struggles for families affected by disability is isolation. Due to the amount of energy and logistical details needed to engage in common community-based activities—such as church, grocery shopping, school, and even a day at the park—far too many families find themselves on an island. As their children grow up, that sense of isolation remains, and many teens, young adults, and older adults find themselves lacking a sense of belonging.

The feeling of not belonging is excruciatingly painful and is often part of the daily lives of individuals affected by disability, as well as their parents, siblings, caregivers, and extended family members. Family members may be so busy in the daily grind that they rarely have time to stop and recognize their isolation, let alone strategize on how to become more involved. When they do make time for community, will they have a local church that loves and embraces them, or will their sense of aloneness be their true reality?

The first step to developing authentic community is to make every reasonable accommodation within your church so that barriers to attendance no longer exist. This includes physical accessibility; but more often than not, it also requires social and emotional accessibility. Do your teaching style, small-group interaction, ministry service opportunities, and general sense of community include or exclude people affected by disability? Will teens with special needs be welcome in your youth group or pushed to the side? Can young adults with disabilities not merely attend but also fully engage in small groups, or are they left to fend for themselves? Where in your church can adults affected by disability gather to talk about God, the Bible, and life without fear of discrimination?

Tackling Real-life Issues

Don't lose sight of the fact that young adults affected by disability are still young adults. Developmentally, they experience many things as they grow into adulthood. They are no longer children. They are no longer teens. They are adults and they should be treated as such.

An effective disability ministry should be willing to tackle real-life issues. These conversations may not be easy to have, but they are vital in helping our friends navigate adulthood. Young adults in this developmental stage will likely be dealing with some, if not all, of the following life issues:

- Learning how to be emotionally healthy
- Navigating new and challenging friendships
- Serving others

- Living independently
- Finding employment or meaningful volunteer opportunities, and managing finances
- Dealing with the death of a loved one

These difficult life issues can be discussed in the context of a one-on-one mentoring relationship, small group, or in your regular ministry setting. Allowing our friends to process these topics with other adults who have experienced these things will increase their sense of community and will give them the opportunity to minister to one another. In addition, it is essential as a ministry leader to be aware of the organizations and resources that are available within your local community. Regional centers, the ARC, civic organizations, and local stores are often wonderful places that provide opportunities for individuals affected by disability to work, volunteer, or receive other valuable support. One component of being an authentic community is engaging in meaningful relationships with your community and helping to build bridges for your friends affected by disability.

Practically, each of the life issues listed above can be developed into a lesson or series of lessons based on the Bible. The Bible has much to say on healthy sexuality, being a good friend, dealing with death, and many other real-life issues. Approaching these topics with honesty and a biblical perspective can be both powerful and engaging. Because it is so relevant to what many of our young adult (and even older adult) friends are experiencing, it may even be more engaging than a study of Bible characters.

Emotional health grounded in Christ

> One of the most heartbreaking realities for an individual with a disability is that far too often they are excluded from the truths of the Bible that define, in very positive ways, who we are. Many people do not think to apply common passages of Scripture to our friends—for example, they are created in the image of God (see Genesis 1); they are created with a purpose (see Exodus 4); they are indispensable to the church (see 1 Corinthians 12). These verses and others like them should impact our friends with disabilities, helping them understand their identity in Christ. As we engage in friendships with individuals with disabilities, we have the unique opportunity

to help them accept their limitations and not compare themselves to others, while also empowering them to set goals and work on areas of growth. With a strong focus on Christ, we can help our friends with disabilities be realistic without squashing their dreams. We can encourage them to focus on the promises of God, the character of God, and their responsibility to trust and obey.

As you help your friends grow in Christ, you will likely have conversations about the disappointments they face and the longings they have for marriage and children, independence, and friendships. You may help them process as they grieve their lack of options and their struggle with feeling excluded. As young adults and adults with disabilities experience the same hormonal fluctuations as everyone else, you may have conversations in which you help them understand the importance of maintaining purity of heart in the midst of sexual temptations.

The best way we can help our friends and loved ones navigate the challenges of life is to point them to Christ. Through our knowledge of Scripture, we gain confidence in Christ and have a better understanding of how to navigate life's challenges. Our friends with special needs are no exception. Similarly, Scripture should also influence how the congregation at large views our friends with disabilities. A biblical perspective on disability should lead to significant change, individually and corporately.

Navigating new and challenging friendships

Friendships with people who have disabilities are too often unchosen and avoided. There is nothing wrong with building a relationship with a person with severe autism, for example. The relationship will likely look different from other relationships someone might have, but that does not mean it is not life-giving and valuable. Some relationships might be thought of as more "customary" in the way that interaction develops. But everyone has different types of relationships with different people. An individual's relationship with his parents will not look the same as that with his siblings or with his co-workers. None of these relationships are impaired; they are simply different.

We encourage you not only to be open to relationships with people affected by disability but also to pursue these friendships. As you do so, we encourage you to set boundaries and stick with them. Our friends with disabilities may experience a greater degree of loneliness and longing for safe and caring relationships. It is important to recognize your friend's needs, but it is also vital to understand that you are only one person who cannot meet all of their needs. By setting and keeping boundaries, you set yourself and your friend up for success rather than unintentional hurt and disappointment.

It can be a great idea to go out in groups, thereby encouraging more friendships outside of yourself. As you do so, you will need to be prepared to accommodate their unique special needs, which may include transportation, accessibility, sensitivity to overstimulation, sounds, foods, movement, and more.

Do your best to keep expectations realistic and communicate openly. It goes without saying that this type of friendship will have uniquechallengesalongwithuniqueblessings.

Independent living

Most everyone desires to live as independently as possible when they enter adulthood. What this looks like can vary widely, but it mostly boils down to being able to make decisions for oneself. To the degree possible, we want to assist our friends in achieving this goal. The church is an incredible network through which people can find places to live and potentially even supports by which to live as independently as possible. Truthfully, these resources have yet to be fully explored and developed in most local churches.

To help develop skills for independent living, we encourage you to check out the local independent living centers in your state. As you learn what options are available, you can discuss with your friend if she is interested in being part of a center where practical life skills are learned, such as handling money, shopping for groceries, washing clothes, cooking, and performing basic personal hygiene. Group homes can also offer practical support while allowing your friend the freedom of living outside the home of her primary caregivers.

If your friend is interested in transitioning from the home of her parents or primary caregivers, be sure to include the family in this conversation. A transition like this will take significant planning and preparation. As a team, you can prayerfully gauge the practicality of your friend living in a group home or on her own in a safe and understanding environment.

Employment, meaningful volunteerism, and financial management

As young adults affected by disability graduate from high school, they are faced with the question of what comes next. For many individuals and families, this unique life stage can produce excessive amounts of anxiety. During the school years, individuals are prepared with skills that should lead to employment. Securing employment in the community post-graduation is encouraged repeatedly and is even expected. In some communities, waiver-based services (supplemental resources that allow individuals affected by disability to continue living at home or in their community instead of at a licensed health facility), such as meal preparation, physical exercise, and personal care, are even withheld until young adults, who are post high school, can prove they have attempted to secure community-based employment (an intentional program designed to provide employment training and rehabilitation services to individuals affected by disability).

Finding employment is easily one of the most pressing issues at this life stage and can also be very difficult for a young adult affected by disability. We believe that the local church can play a significant role in alleviating some of this pressure. What if the church opened its doors Monday through Friday for things like volunteering, job training, part-time employment, or even full-time employment? There are many tasks within the walls of the church that could easily be done by young adults affected by disability. Basic office work, facility maintenance, visitor phone calls, and staff encouragement are examples of wonderful opportunities that could be made available to people affected by disability. As the church seeks to be a blessing, it may just be surprised by how much it is blessed.

Dealing with grief and the loss of loved ones

A loss of any kind can be a life-changing event. As we age and experience life, we face the inevitable reality that we will experience loss and grief through varying circumstances or death. It takes time to sort through feelings of depression and anger. This is a reality that all people face, regardless of their abilities or disabilities. As we support our friends in seasons of loss, it is important to leave time for asking why, for grief, for pain to subside, and for acceptance to come. We wish we could provide easy tips on easing this adjustment period, but we can only encourage you to be a good listener and a strong support to your friend during this difficult period, offering advice and counsel only sparingly.

Whenever we face loss, we are reminded that prayer is always the most powerful instrument of change in an individual's life. Galatians 6:2 tells us to "bear one other's burdens"—your presence and your friendship can do just that. We are confident that your actions of care and concern will lay a proper foundation for further sharing as the process of grieving unfolds.

As you work through these practical life issues, we encourage you to be strategic in your approach. It is important to do more than just preach at our friends affected by disability. There are many websites and local centers that can also assist practically in the navigation of these topics. Giving your friends the opportunity to discuss these challenging subjects with the loving guidance of a leader will allow them to take more ownership over the concepts and build each other up. As we previously mentioned, our goal is to encourage our friends to step into ministry with others. By encouraging them to participate and not just listen, they will be better equipped to serve others.

Mentoring

We believe that mentoring is one of the ways that you can have the greatest amount of impact in your ministry with individuals affected by disability. Many leaders shy away from mentoring because it tends to be individualized and non-programmatic. It can also be time-consuming and difficult to do on a large scale. But allow us to share our thoughts on what mentoring is and is not, and why we feel it is an important component of ministry with youth and adults affected by disability.

1. *Mentoring is an intentional act.* It is not something that happens by accident. Effective leaders should be consistently looking for people to connect with and invest in on a personal level. While there may be times when an individual approaches you and asks to be mentored, more often mentoring begins with an invitation into the process.
2. *Mentoring is time-consuming.* Healthy mentoring cannot happen in short-lived moments. It takes a commitment and an investment into the life of another person.

3. *Mentoring can change someone's life trajectory.* We all need others who believe in us. There are countless stories of the difference that one person made when they chose to see the good and potential in somebody else. Consider the life transformation that happened when Mr. Miyagi invested in Daniel LaRusso's life and changed him from being a young man throwing his life away and into the Karate Kid. Or look at the example of the apostle Paul, who poured into Timothy, encouraging him to become all that God was calling him to be. Who has God placed in your life whom you can intentionally encourage and mentor?
4. *Mentoring is not a one-way street.* You may think you are there to help and guide your mentee, but you will soon realize that you have much to learn as well. Mentoring is also not about you turning your friend with disability into you. It is about you helping your friend become who God created her to be. As with everything else in life and ministry, relationship matters. In order to mentor others, you do not need to have all the answers.

We believe that through the process, you will be challenged, encouraged and inspired as much as your mentee is.

5. *Mentoring is not complex.* It is simply intentional relationship. In a mentoring relationship, we make time for each other with the specific goal of helping someone take the next step, whatever that step might be. Do your best to avoid overcomplicating the process.

For mentoring to be truly successful, it is important to see the potential in others, to root for their success, and to always believe the best about them. Without this, the process of mentoring can unfortunately become more of a task and obligation than a joy-filled opportunity. The following steps can be used as a basic guide for an effective mentoring relationship.

The first step, after establishing a mutual desire for a mentoring relationship, is to clarify goals, roles, and expectations. What is the purpose of this mentoring opportunity? What specific goals do you or your mentee have in mind? What are the hopes and dreams of the individual you plan to mentor? How often will you meet, and what will this look like? Will it be in person, on the phone, through video conferencing, or something completely different? Mentoring relationships are generally more successful if all these details are clearly communicated up front. It allows everybody to know what is involved, how much investment is being made, and how long the relationship will potentially last.

Once all the details have been sorted out, it is essential to obtain a certain level of commitment. Mentoring requires regular conversations, regular interactions, and regular moments of redirecting. Without commitment, it becomes virtually impossible to see growth through mentoring. As you move through the mentoring process, you will be in a constant cycle of assessment and appreciation. You must look at current activities in light of the established goals and then measure the progress. Generally speaking, most people are more motivated to grow within a culture of appreciation than in a culture of criticism. Look for and capitalize upon every opportunity to celebrate each milestone.

One aspect of mentoring that is necessary but often difficult is the need to challenge the status quo. You will help your mentee succeed as you gently encourage him to try new things, go new places, and embark on new adventures. Growth cannot happen within a bubble, and mentors must be willing to bring an expectation of appropriate progress to the relationship. This gentle pushing must be handled with wisdom. You do not want to create an environment of fear and insecurity as this can lead to a stunting of the mentoring process. While you are challenging the status quo, you also want to set up your friend for success. Be there to pick him up if he falls, to encourage him when he comes up short, and, if necessary, to completely redirect him when the current course of action is not moving him closer to the agreed-upon goals.

In mentoring you may see grand results or you may only see small results. Please don't ever wonder if the small results are worth it. Small results now can have tremendous impact later. Mentoring is worth the investment, no matter the size of the change. We are simply called to invest; God will determine the results.

When you choose to mentor a young adult with a disability, you are taking a chance on someone. God loves that person dearly and has specific plans for her life. By mentoring, you have the potential to change someone's life trajectory. By mentoring, you could empower someone to become who God has created her to be. You could release her to *do* ministry and not just be an object *of* ministry.

Ready to Launch?

Ministry is messy. Life gets challenging and difficult and frustrating at times. As you lead and build authentic community with teens and adults affected by disability, you must keep in mind that life is often even more overwhelming for them. Depending upon the nature of their disability and the severity, there might simply be tasks and activities that they are unable to engage in. This can lead them to feel a sense of loss, a lack of value—and even to wonder what is wrong with them. As you move beyond buddy ministry, remember that God is calling you to be a friend, a mentor, and a partner on this wonderful journey called life. From puberty to college to employment options and beyond, life is complicated in a wonderfully enjoyable way, and it is a privilege to come alongside friends affected by disability and see them reach the hopes and dreams that God has in store for them.

As you lead in this arena of ministry, keep in mind that we are all much more similar than we are different. Allow disability to be a unique identifier but not a relational hindrance. Our prayer is that you see all people through the eyes of God, remind them that they are fearfully and wonderfully made (see Psalm 139:14), and enjoy the journey of life together. Teen and adult ministries present different challenges and opportunities than buddy ministry does, but these are challenges and opportunities that allow God to shine as your friends affected by disability know him in a more personal way and experience life as he intended. Blessings upon you, your team, and your church as you prepare to launch into the wonderful world of teen and adult ministry for people affected by disability!

Becoming ***Irresistible***

Luke 14 commands Christ followers to "Go quickly . . . find the blind, the lame, and the crippled . . . and compel them to come in!" While this sounds inspiring and daunting, exciting and overwhelming, motivating and frightening, all at the same time, what does it actually mean? How do we live and function within the church in such a way that families affected by disability are compelled to walk through our doors to experience the body of Christ?

We can certainly *compel* them by offering programs, ministries, events, and other church activities, but what if the compelling aspect was more about heart, culture, acceptance and embracing? What if our churches were overflowing with the hope of Jesus Christ . . . a hope not simply for those who "fit in" or look the part, but rather a hope to all, including the marginalized, downtrodden and outcast?

Becoming *Irresistible* is more than programs and activities–it is about a transformational work in our hearts . . . first as individuals and then as the body of Christ. *Irresistible* allows us to see each individual as he or she truly is: created in the image of God (Genesis 1:26-27), designed purposely as a masterpiece (Psalm 139:13-14), instilled with purpose, plans and dreams (Jeremiah 29:11), and a truly indispensable member of the kingdom of God (1 Corinthians 12:23). An *Irresistible Church* is an "authentic community built on the hope of Christ that compels people affected by disability to fully belong." It is powerful for a person to know that he or she is fully welcomed and belongs. *Irresistible* captures the heart of the church as it should be—how else do we explain the rapid growth and intense attraction to the church in the book of Acts? The heart of God was embodied through the people of God by the Spirit of God . . . and that is simply *Irresistible*!

The Irresistible Church Series is designed to help not only shape and transform the heart of the church, but also to provide the practical steps and activities to put *flesh* around the *heart* of the church—to help your church become a place for people to fully belong. Thank you for responding to the call to become *Irresistible*. It will not happen overnight, but it will happen. As with all good things, it requires patience and perseverance, determination and dedication, and ultimately an underlying trust in the faithfulness of God. May God bless you on this journey. Be assured that you are not alone—there are many on the path of *Irresistible*.

For more information or to join the community,
please visit www.irresistiblechurch.org.

Joni and Friends
INTERNATIONAL DISABILITY CENTER

Joni and Friends was established in 1979 by Joni Eareckson Tada, who at 17 was injured in a diving accident, leaving her a quadriplegic. Since its inception, Joni and Friends has been dedicated to extending the love and message of Christ to people who are affected by disability whether it is the disabled person, a family member, or friend. Our objective is to meet the physical, emotional, and spiritual needs of this group of people in practical ways.

Joni and Friends is committed to recruiting, training, and motivating new generations of people with disabilities to become leaders in their churches and communities. Today, the Joni and Friends International Disability Center serves as the administrative hub for an array of programs which provide outreach to thousands of families affected by disability around the globe. These include two radio programs, an award-winning television series, the Wheels for the World international wheelchair distribution ministry, Family Retreats which provide respite for those with disabilities and their families, Field Services to provide church training along with educational and inspirational resources at a local level, and the Christian Institute on Disability to establish a firm biblical worldview on disability-related issues.

From local neighborhoods to the far reaches of the world, Joni and Friends is striving to demonstrate to people affected by disability, in tangible ways, that God has not abandoned them—he is with them—providing love, hope, and eternal salvation.

Available Now in the Irresistible Church Series

Start with Hello

Introducing Your Church to Special Needs Ministry

Families with special needs often share that they desire two things in their church: accessibility and acceptance. Accessibility to existing structures, programs and people is an imperative. Acceptance with a sense of belonging by the others who also participate in the structures, programs and fellowship of the church is equally necessary. In this simple book you'll learn the five steps to becoming an accessible and accepting church.

To receive first notice of upcoming resources, including respite, inclusive worship and support groups, please contact us at churchrelations@joniandfriends.org.

Available Now in the Irresistible Church Series

We've Got This!

Providing Respite for Families Affected by Disability

Families or caregivers who have children with disabilities are often isolated, exhausted, and grieving. Respite events can be a safe bridge for families to cross over the threshold of the church by satisfying an urgent need. A place for children to be themselves, for caregivers to have a break and for the church to serve well is invaluable. This book is a practical guide that provides the necessary tools to plan and execute a successful respite event.

To receive first notice of upcoming resources, including respite, inclusive worship and support groups, please contact us at churchrelations@joniandfriends.org.

Available Now in the Irresistible Church Series

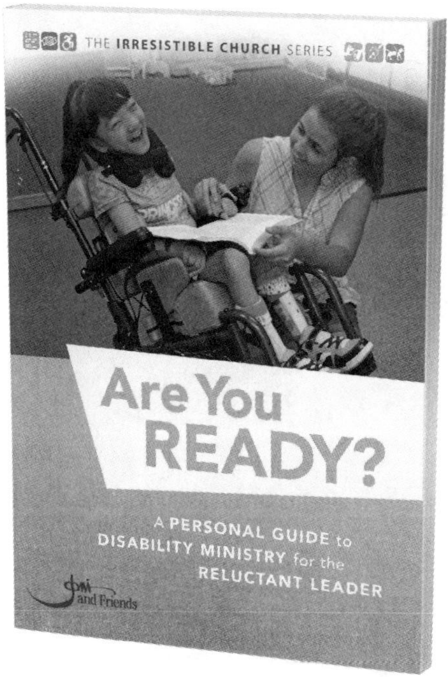

Are You Ready

A Personal Guide to Disability Ministry for the Reluctant Leader

Does the thought of engaging in disability ministry make you nervous? Are you unclear on how to lead others as you serve and embrace individuals affected by disability? As you read the pages of this book, you will learn the biblical perspective regarding disability, consider both the heart of a leader and the heart of the church, and begin to recognize and serve your community's practical needs. Together, you and your team will see the development and growth of a truly Irresistible Church.

To receive first notice of upcoming resources, including respite, inclusive worship and support groups, please contact us at churchrelations@joniandfriends.org.

Available Now in the Irresistible Church Series

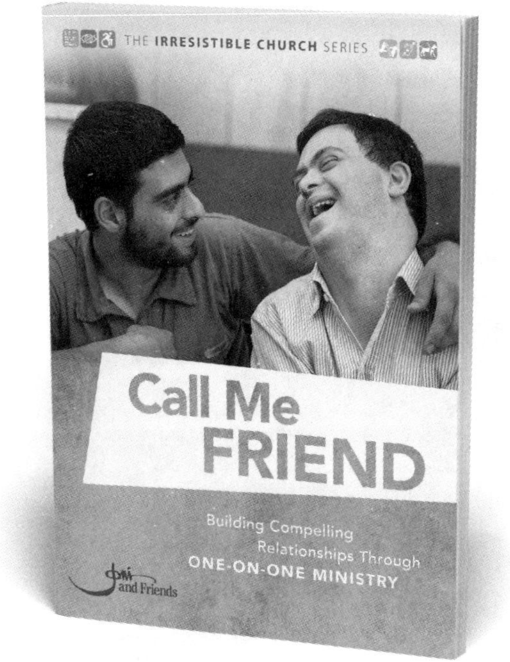

Call Me Friend

Building Compelling Relationships Through One-on-One Ministry

For the ministry leader who desires to include people of all ages with special needs in the life of the church, this practical guide to buddy ministry provides clear, concise direction on how to organize and implement this effective ministry model. Leaders will discover how buddies provide discipleship, friendship, safety, participation, communication and positive behavior management. The simple steps you'll find in this book will build relationships and assist your church in becoming an authentic community where all people may fully belong.

To receive first notice of upcoming resources, including respite, inclusive worship and support groups, please contact us at churchrelations@joniandfriends.org.

Available Now in the Irresistible Church Series

Pathways to Belonging

Creating Inclusive Ministry Environments for All Ages

Church leaders with a heart to serve families affected by disability frequently ask, "How do I know the best way to include each special friend when their needs vary?" This book is a response to that question, offering step-by-step tools for evaluating the needs of friends with disabilities and creating a culture that welcomes these individuals and their families. Within these pages, we discuss creating accessible environments that provide access to the gospel while being sensitive to learning styles and physical needs.

To receive first notice of upcoming resources, including respite, inclusive worship and support groups, please contact us at churchrelations@joniandfriends.org.

Available Now in the Irresistible Church Series

Shout for JOY!

Engaging the Whole Church in Accessible Worship

Do you long to be part of a church community where people of all abilities gather to worship, a church where the sounds of worship include a wheelchair rolling down the aisle, the tap of a cane, and the sound of people with differing intellectual disabilities lifting their voices together in praise and prayer? If so, we pray that *Shout for Joy!* will help your church have a heart for worship that is accessible to all and give you some practical "how-to" ideas as well.

To receive first notice of upcoming resources, including respite, inclusive worship and support groups, please contact us at churchrelations@joniandfriends.org.

Available Now in the Irresistible Church Series

Go Make Disciples

Embracing People Affected by Disability Through Mentoring Relationships

Irresistible leadership is not merely about leading individuals affected by disability. Rather, it is about creating space for everybody who is called into leadership to come, grow, and express their gifts and talents. Healthy leadership does not happen *to* people affected by disability, nor does it only happen *for* them. It should happen *with* them. Learn the four steps to a healthy mentoring relationship and be used by God to release people into the spheres of leadership where he has called them..

To receive first notice of upcoming resources, including respite, inclusive worship and support groups, please contact us at churchrelations@joniandfriends.org.

Other Recommended Resources

Beyond Suffering Bible

The *Beyond Suffering Bible* by Joni and Friends is the first study Bible made specifically for those who suffer and the people who love them. Uplifting insights from Joni Eareckson Tada and numerous experts and scholars who have experienced suffering in their own lives and will help you move beyond the "why" of suffering to grasp the eternal value God is building into our lives. Special features include: inspiring devotionals, biblical and contemporary profiles, Bible reading plans, connection points and disability ministry resources.

Find out more at http://www.joniandfriends.org/store/category/bibles/

Beyond Suffering® Student Edition

Beyond Suffering for the Next Generation: A Christian View on Disability Ministry will equip young people to consider the issues that affect people with disabilities and their families, and inspire them to action. Students who embrace this study will gain confidence to join a growing, worldwide movement that God is orchestrating to fulfill Luke 14:21-23: "Go out quickly into the streets and alleys of the town and bring in the poor, the crippled, the blind, and the lame.... so that my house will be full."

ISBN: 978-0-9838484-6-2
304 pages · 8.5″ x 11″
Includes CD-ROM

Joni: An Unforgettable Story

In this unforgettable autobiography, Joni reveals each step of her struggle to accept her disability and discover the meaning of her life. The hard-earned truths she discovers and the special ways God reveals his love are testimonies to faith's triumph over hardship and suffering. This new edition includes an afterword, in which Joni talks about the events that have occurred in her life since the book's original publication in 1976, including her marriage and the expansion of her worldwide ministry to families affected by disability.

ISBN: 978-0310240013
205 pages · Paperback

www.joniandfriends.org · P.O. Box 3333, Agoura Hills, CA 91376
(818) 707-5664 · Fax: (818) 707-2391 TTY: (818) 707-9707

Customizable Resources from the Book

Available for Download at

http://www.irresistiblechurch.org/library

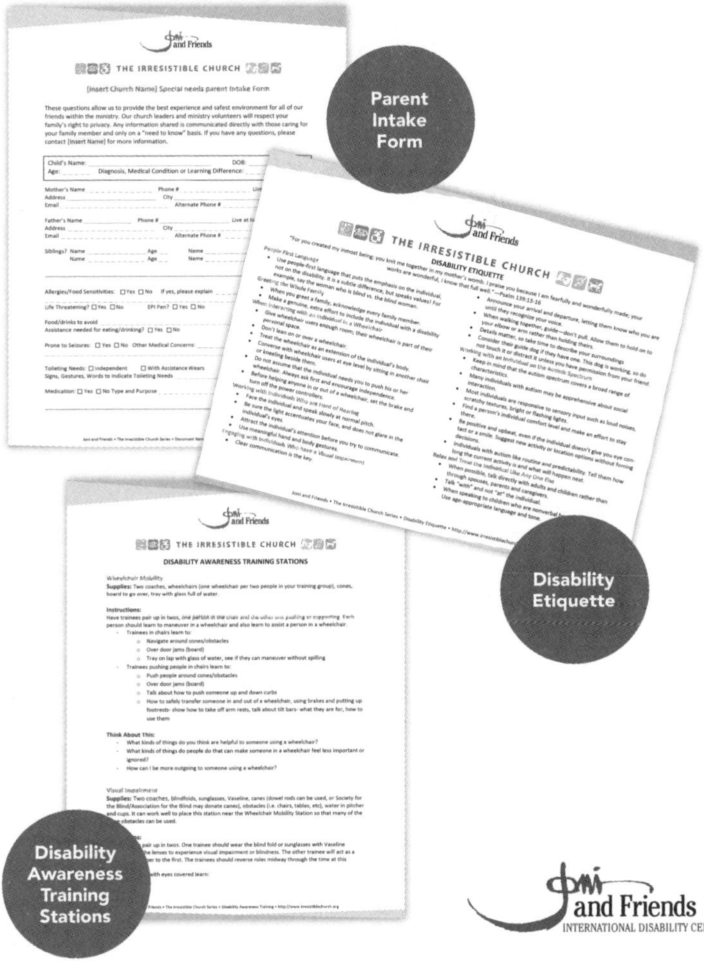

Joni and Friends

INTERNATIONAL DISABILITY CENTER